BEARING WITNESS

GENOCIDE AND ETHNIC CLEANSING™

THE GUATEMALAN
GENOCIDE OF THE MAYA PEOPLE

JOHN A. TORRES

Rosen
YA™

NEW YORK

Published in 2018 by The Rosen Publishing Group, Inc.
29 East 21st Street, New York, NY 10010

Library of Congress Cataloging-in-Publication Data

Names: Torres, John Albert, author.
Title: The Guatemalan genocide of the Maya people / John A. Torres.
Description: New York : Rosen Publishing, 2018. | Series: Bearing witness : genocide and ethnic cleansing | Audience: Grades 7–12. | Includes bibliographical references and index.
Identifiers: LCCN 2017017237 | ISBN 9781508177364 (library bound) | ISBN 9781508178705 (paperback)
Subjects: LCSH: Mayas—Crimes against—Guatemala—History—20th century—Juvenile literature. | Mayas—Guatemala—Government relations—Juvenile literature. | Mayas—Guatemala—History—Juvenile literature. | Genocide—Guatemala—History—Juvenile literature. | Guatemala—Ethnic relations—History—Juvenile literature. | Guatemala—Politics and government—Juvenile literature.
Classification: LCC F1435.3.C75 T67 2018 | DDC 972.81—dc23
LC record available at https://lccn.loc.gov/2017017237

Manufactured in China

On the cover: In 2001, Guatemalan Maya Quiche Indian women memorialize forty-one victims whose coffins were found after the episode of genocide that the Guatemalan government committed against their people.

CONTENTS

INTRODUCTION

The term "genocide" was not used until 1944 after the Nazi atrocities of World War II were discovered. Genocide refers to the systematic and deliberate killing of a large group of people, typically in one ethnic group or religious faith. During World War II, German authorities tried to eliminate the Jews. They succeeded in killing six million people, the vast majority of whom were Jewish (disabled people, other minorities, and gay people were also targeted). This instance of genocide came to be known as the Holocaust.

This is an artist's depiction of what a typical Mayan city looked like. Note the temple at the center of the square.

Instances of genocide and ethnic cleansing have become even more essential to study. Genocide and ethnic cleansing have taken place all over the world. Examples of recent incidents include Hutus killing almost a million Tutsis in Rwanda in 1994. In 2014 in Iraq, ISIS chased fifty thousand Yazidis up Sinjar Mountain to leave them to starve to death and slaughtered five thousand who didn't flee. ISIS also enslaved thousands of women and girls that they captured. The Yazidis aren't safe from ISIS yet. Syria's crisis is more difficult to define, as it is too dangerous for watchdog groups to get close enough to offer a count that demonstrates the impact. The hatred and anger that can cause one group to mercilessly attack another generally unfolds in a predictable pattern, but the pattern is only predictable to those who intentionally observe the events that lead up to the killings and aggression.

Such is the story of the Mayans.

Mayans were once at the forefront of civilization before they were wiped off the earth. They were ahead of their time regarding language, writing, mathematics, calendars, and other aspects of education and technology. Examples of their magnificent architecture, temples, and towers still stand today.

Describing the Mayan civilization as mysterious is an understatement. There are as many questions about the rise of the Mayans in Mesoamerica as there are about their sudden decline. But examining the rise of the Mayan civilization and the many theories developed to explain its sudden and shocking decline and disappearance can help to shed light on what went wrong.

Famine, war, disease, or something even more sinister was brewing in the Mayans' backyard. It is clear to historians that entire cities, complete with hospitals, schools, and sporting arenas, were abandoned, but they don't know why. Maybe their belief and devotion to a set of gods that were tied to nature made them afraid and caused them to simply walk away from their homes. Or maybe they were forced away or killed.

Examining the nature of the Mayans may offer some answers. The early scholars believed the Mayans were a peaceful people, but they were proved wrong. There are some indications that old treaties and alliances were no longer in effect and that city-states within the Mayan empire itself may have gone to war with one another. Their enemies could have come in and wiped them out, or it is possible that the Mayans themselves were successful in killing each other. Ultimately, all historians know for sure is that a modern-day genocide of these ancient people took place just a few decades ago.

CHAPTER 1

THE RISE OF THE MAYAN EMPIRE

In order to understand what happened to the Mayans, knowing how they came to be and what they did to thrive adds perspective to their story. This helps explain the implications of the historical episode that ended with an attempt to rid the world of them.

A VAST EXPANSE OF LAND

Thousands of years before the civilization known as the Mayan Empire came to be, the first hunter-gatherers came to settle in the area that would later be known as the Maya lowlands and highlands in Mesoamerica.

This region would become invaluable over the centuries to anthropologists, archaeologists, and others who studied ancient histories and civilizations. Mesoamerica would, at one time or another, be home to the following ancient civilizations: the Aztec, Purépecha, Olmec, Teotihuacan, and Maya.

This massive area of Mesoamerica, which literally means Middle America, is a vast expanse of land that extends from the southern part of North America down into Central America. It would cover the southern half of Mexico, Guatemala, Belize, Honduras, El Salvador, and Nicaragua. Most historians divide Mesoamerica up into the lowlands and the highlands.

It is important to note that it is rare for a civilization to exist and even thrive in such different regions and climates. These hunter-gatherers, who would later make up the foundation of the Mayan civilization, were able to thrive in subtropical jungle climates, rainforests, dry arid areas, and even the colder mountainous regions. Most of the ancient civilizations were

This is a modern map of Central America and the Caribbean islands. The area known as Mesoamerica resided in and between Mexico and Nicaragua.

founded in dryer climates and would thrive as long as fresh water was available nearby.

Most agree that the time period around 2600 BCE is around when the Mayan civilization came to be. Archaeologists have found that it was during this time that many small settlements began to take shape and eventually grow into cities. The main industry was farming as the people learned how to grow and cultivate crops like beans, squash, and corn. They also learned to make tools out of clay.

As the settlements grew into cities, the Mayan people developed a written language that would spread throughout the area. They would also begin to build large and very impressive structures.

AN EMPIRE CONTINUES TO GROW

The next era of the Mayan Empire is regarded as the Classic Period (250 CE–900 CE). The Mayan people would develop a type of calendar that was based on a 365-day year like the Gregorian calendar to mark time. This is also when they constructed large towers, temples, and other monuments that would rival that of many other great ancient civilizations. Because of this, some refer to this era as the Mayan Empire's Golden Age.

This was a period that was also marked by artistic and intellectual advancements that saw the construction of schools and even sporting arenas, where some speculate sports were played using a ball.

THE MAYAN CALENDAR

The Mayan Calendar refers to a system of calendars that the Mayans developed and used to mark time. Legend has it that the Mayan god Itzamna gave the people the knowledge of calendars as well as the gift of writing. Itzamna was the highest and most powerful of the Mayan gods.

The Mayans' way of marking time in calendars like the one pictured h[ere] is one of their most enduring gifts to humankind.

The Mayan calendar uses three different lengths of time. The first is a count of 260 days that is called the Tzolk'in. This was then used in conjunction with the 365-day solar year known as Haab'. Then another calendar, known as the Long Count, was used to track very long periods of time.

The Mayan calendar is still used today by many of the Mayans who live in the highlands of Guatemala. The calendars are often round and designed with ornate depictions of their gods. Some of the calendars even used lunar cycles in their methodology.

The Mayan calendar was sometimes used by eschatologists to predict the end of time. Some believed the end of the world would happen in 2003 because that was when the Mayan calendar seemed to end. But then another interpretation moved it to 2012. Many people throughout the world had "end-of-the-world parties" to commemorate the end of the calendar.

What is truly impressive is that the civilization grew to include roughly forty cities. Some were not more than small settlements of about five thousand people while the largest were home to fifty thousand people. During the Classic Period, the population was believed to be more than two million people.

The cities, large or small, contained many of the same elements. They had palaces or community centers, plazas, and temples. Almost all of the cities were surrounded by farms that probably supplied the city with food and other cities within the growing empire with goods to trade. These farmers were believed to have employed several modern-day farming techniques, including irrigation and terracing.

Among these cities were Tikal, Calakmul, Bonampak, and more. But no city during this time would be more important than that of Teotihuacan, which would serve as the unofficial capital of the empire for several generations. Teotihuacan existed near modern-day Mexico City. It was often the rulers of Teotihuacan who would have the final say over what king or tribal chief would rule over a particular city.

These Mayan ruins in Chiapas, Mexico, have withstood time and have been successfully restored. Note the large grassy field where the Mayans probably enjoyed a variety of sporting events.

Like many ancient civilizations, the Mayan people were very religious and would worship different gods. There were gods of the sun, moon, fire, rain, crops, and other areas of nature. And like many ancient cultures, the Mayans believed that their kings or rulers—known as *kuhul ajaw*, or holy lords—were also descendants of the gods. The people believed their rulers spoke to the gods and could intercede or mediate on their behalf. These rulers were also responsible for performing very detailed religious ceremonies that were very important to everyday life for the Mayans.

UNEASY ALLIANCES

The rulers of Mayan cities were also charged with keeping the peace and negotiating treaties and alliances between cities. Historians say this is similar to how the city-states of classic Greece or Renaissance-era Italy operated.

These alliances were not always easy. The strongest and largest forces were certainly able to impose their will on smaller cities and regions. However, it was seen as a matter of great pride and prestige for a small city to enter into an agreement or alliance with one of the larger, more powerful cities. It really was a civilization built on allies and vassals.

The elaborate temples built to honor the gods and perform religious ceremonies were similar to the pyramids of ancient Egypt. Because the Mayans became so adept at chiseling inscriptions in these rock structures, archaeologists were able to learn about them. However, it was not until the mid-twentieth century that the Mayan hieroglyphic system of writing was deciphered.

The Mayans learned how to make paper out of tree bark and they became prolific writers, with apparently thousands of folding manuscripts. However, only four of these texts have survived and experts are still trying to decipher exactly what they mean. Experts believe that Mayan holy men used these texts during religious rituals.

Unfortunately, Spanish explorers and conquistadores—influenced by the Catholic Church, which wanted to convert the Mayans—destroyed the vast majority of the manuscripts. They called them "superstitious" and "evil."

Some of the Mayan ruins that survive today, like Tikal National Park in Guatemala, are incredible examples of their architectural brilliance.

The Mayans were very advanced when it came to mathematics and astronomy. In fact, they were one of the first people to use zero in mathematics, mainly as a placeholder while doing equations.

By the year 500 CE, the city of Tikal had grown and become the unofficial capital of the empire. Teotihuacan would not last much longer as an important part of the Mayan Empire. Tikal was located much farther south than Teotihuacan, in what is now modern-day Guatemala. Tikal was rare because it was one of the few major cities located in the heart of El Petén rainforest. The occupants were able to use nearby rivers in order to travel to other areas and sell and trade their goods.

At its height, Tikal was home to almost one hundred thousand people The city grew for hundreds of years and added infrastructure that would rival any other great ancient city.

But, like much of the Mayan Empire, it collapsed just as quickly as it rose to power.

CHAPTER 2

THE START OF THE DECLINE

By the time the would-be conquerors from Spain arrived in the sixteenth century, many of the great Mayan cities had already been abandoned. Why and how such a great civilization suddenly ceased to exist is a great mystery. However, it is clear that some of the Mayans' activities may have contributed to their initial decline.

BLOOD AND SACRIFICE

Blood and sacrifices were an important part of Mayan life. The Mayans believed that they had to nourish the gods to keep them strong. They believed that the only way to do that was with human blood. In fact, humans were regularly sacrificed in Mayan cities.

These human sacrifices were often very violent. The two most popular methods were by beheading the sacrifice or removing the person's heart while they were still alive. Other methods included a firing squad of arrows. Another method involved tossing the victim into a pit or a sinkhole and letting them starve to death. Perhaps the most graphic method of human sacrifice involved tying the victims' hands up over their head and disemboweling them— while they were still alive. Sometimes the heads of the decapitated victims would be used as balls during sporting events.

This 2007 color lithograph portrays the sometimes brutal nature of the Mayan rituals. Those rituals often included blood sacrifice.

They would often practice self-mutilation and bloodletting as well. They often drained themselves of enough blood to experience hallucinations. They believed these hallucinations were a way to contact the gods or the spirits of dead relatives.

Archaeologists have discovered many of these methods carved into ancient Mayan artifacts collected over the years.

BLOOD BAKERIES

Blood was extremely important to the everyday life of the Mayan people. Blood sacrifices to the gods and rituals involving blood occurred everyday. They were a regular part of Mayan life.

While it is clear that the Mayans believed their gods demanded blood sacrifices in order to keep order in the universe, it is also clear that royal blood was looked at as more valuable than animal blood or that of a commoner. In fact, sometimes royal blood was offered to the common people as a treat or as a way to get closer to the gods. Sometimes the blood was smeared on paper and then burned so that the smoke could reach the heavens and please the gods. On certain religious holidays throughout the year, the royalty would pierce certain parts of their bodies and collect the blood. It would then be smeared or poured on maize, or corn. The corn would be baked into a special kind of bread, known as sacred bread. This bread was believed to have special powers, especially as a fertilizer and for improving fertility.

CONTINUING THE TRADITION

The Mayans participated in some particularly destructive practices. They inflicted these practices on themselves and surrounding communities.

The Mayans may have felt constant pressure to appease the bloodthirsty gods. Since the Mayans also believed their rulers were descendants of the gods, these rulers often demanded blood sacrifices as well. Perhaps the people did not always want to offer up their own denizens. In this case, the Mayans could save themselves by ambushing residents of other cities. They could bring them back to their temples and keep them locked up in order to have a steady supply of victims to sacrifice.

If this theory is true, then this would keep the Mayan cities from helping each other during difficult times, and alliances, cooperation, and agreements would crumble.

This seventh-century artwork portrays Quetzalcoatl, a Mayan deity. The Mayans paid tribute to this god and others for protection.

It was also common practice to try and capture other rulers. It was done with such frequency that there are depictions carved into ancient ruins of one leader or another being led away in humiliation or even being crushed under the weight of a foot.

These ambushes and retaliations often led to prolonged periods of warfare between cities. This not only taxed a city's material resources like food, wood and weapons, but also depleted its male population. This may have meant a shortage of farmers, soldiers, and other workers.

SELF-DESTRUCTING MAYANS

Recent years have revealed evidence for several plausible theories concerning the Mayans' decline. Arthur A. Demarest, an archaeologist at Vanderbilt University, has his own theory. If there was eventually a shortage of commoners in society as more and more people claimed nobility or royal bloodlines, the decline of the Mayans could even have been a case of being under the rule of too many chiefs. He described the Mayans as one of the most violent societies of the new world.

Demarest spent years studying an area in Guatemala that was home to six major Mayan cities and numerous villages. The curious thing that Demarest concluded was that abandoned cities were never destroyed or damaged. His theory concerning the abandoned cities is that conquering factions would either take prisoners or force the people to abandon cities. They had no interest in taking over the conquered cities for themselves or destroying them in a show of force.

It is believed that these long periods of warfare were a factor in the decline of Mayan cities. Quick and frequent changes in leadership could cause a city or region to become unstable. That could lead to the downfall and decline of a civilization. In the case of the Mayan Empire, some cities were conquered and abandoned immediately by fleeing survivors. The constant

This fresco at the Bonampak archaeological site in Chiapas, Mexico, portrays the Mayans waging war with an enemy.

warfare would also play a part in the overall demise of the society, even for the cities that were victorious in these conflicts.

As archaeologists and historians continue to discover new sites, there is more and more evidence that warfare had become not only common but escalated to full-on war. They point to newly discovered archaeological sites in present-day Guatemala that show hastily built walls and fortifications around the city and around important buildings like the temples. The archaeologists were able to identify a clear difference between the carefully constructed buildings of the city and the protective walls. They saw that the walls were built in a hurry by worried or frightened people expecting an attack from their enemies.

THE COST OF WAR

Understanding the collapse and disappearance of the Mayan Empire requires a holistic approach. There likely was not one major cause but several that combined to cause the decline of this civilization.

There is a two-fold negative effect from the fact that merchants would no longer feel safe traveling through areas where active warfare was going on. Not only would this cessation of movement prevent valuable, necessary commodities from making it to the people who needed them, but this would also stop the sharing of information and ideas. Without this free exchange of ideas, societies can become stagnant. Societies could become unwilling to try new things or to experiment with change.

While the violence, warfare, and human sacrifice of the Mayans against one another does not qualify as genocide because of their uniformity of ethnicity and religion, it clearly indicates that violence was likely one of the factors that led to the downfall of the Mayans.

Recent discoveries of Mayan archaeological sites in present-day Guatemala indicate that warfare may have stopped the farmers from producing the food that fed their society. That could easily contribute to a collective death by starvation.

CHAPTER 3

THE DROUGHT AND THE FAMINE

In spite of the Mayans' propensity for violence and war, they thrived as a society under socially adverse conditions for a long time. It is thus likely that it took more than their continuous violent conflicts to end their prosperity. This is where Mother Nature enters the story.

DECLINING RAINFALL

Researchers and archaeologists conducting a 2012 study at Arizona State University spent years studying the Yucatán Peninsula looking for the environmental conditions during the time period of the decline of the Mayans. What they found were indications that the region was suffering a terrible drought. They also found that massive deforestation had taken place.

Another study, done around the same time by Columbia University experts, took a close look at rainfall during that time. They studied mineral deposits left behind by the water that drips in caves. They were able to go back nearly two thousand years and predict what the weather was like back then.

Both theories are based on the knowledge that weather patterns are cyclical. In other words, some regions of the world might be able to expect warmer winters every few decades. These intertwined findings would have a terrible impact on the Mayans.

What the Columbia University team theorized was that the areas occupied by the Mayans enjoyed an unusually long period of rainfall and wet weather just as the civilization was starting to make its mark. This allowed for rich, fertile farmlands, healthy forests, and lots of animals in those forests to hunt and eat. The Mayans were adept at hunting herds of white-tailed deer for food. This meant there was an abundance of food and the population was not only able to thrive but also to grow rapidly. But there is a chance this growth resulted in too many people for the land to sustain.

More people meant building more buildings and clearing more land for farming. The Mayans were experts at constructing massive temples and beautiful structures for their cities. They built with a material called lime plaster. But this material needed to be heated and cooked before it could be used. According to archaeologists, it would have taken twenty full-grown trees to produce only one square meter (ten square feet) of building material for their cities. That means massive amounts of trees were being cut down to help keep up with the population.

The Arizona State University researchers found that deforestation may have caused the soil to erode and become

This is a corridor of the palace at Palenque, a Mayan city-state. Its survival serves as a testament to the Mayans' ingenuity.

depleted. This meant that farmers had a more difficult time growing crops, so they would then simply chop down even more trees for new farming land. This massive clearing of forest likely affected rain patterns because cleared land absorbs less sun and allows less water to evaporate. Less water evaporating from the surface means fewer clouds in the sky and much less rainfall. Chopping down trees limited the amount of rain that would fall. Less rain meant crop failures. Less soil meant that farmers continuously planted in the same fields instead of letting a field recover and replenish the nutrients the soil needed to grow food. Ultimately, fewer trees meant less food.

This happened slowly over time, and no one knows for sure how the people responded. Historians think the Mayans may have slowly started leaving the cities where food was scarce and settled in other less populated areas, away from city life. Such migration would've caused social upheaval.

MALNUTRITION AND DISEASE

It may be possible that food scarcity resulted in more warfare as cities attacked others to eliminate the competition for land and resources. More warfare means that farmers would clear more forests to plant their crops. This would further erode the situation. Famine might have also caused the peasants to riot and revolt against their rulers and to abandon the gods that were supposed to be protecting them.

Scientists who studied the bones of the ancient Mayans have found one basic theme: the Mayan people suffered from extreme malnutrition. They were not getting food and certainly not getting the nutrients their bodies needed. This especially affected children and babies. There have been caves and mass graves found with hundreds of bones of babies and children. Examination of these bones found that the children not only suffered from malnutrition but also anemia, a condition caused by a deficiency of iron in the blood, or caused by a loss of blood. This widespread hunger and malnutrition would have lowered the Mayans' ability to resist disease and made them susceptible to getting sick.

Another disease popped up around this time that is believed to have been another root cause of the disappearance of the Mayans. But this disease is not a human one. A study in 1979 theorized that maize mosaic virus likely occurred during the decline of the Mayan Empire. This disease, which affects corn crops in the Caribbean and South and Central America, is spread by planthoppers and causes the maize crop to yield much less food or fail if the virus is not contained.

These aphids are vectors of the maize mosaic virus microbe. Their contact with Mayan maize crops caused the virus to spread to the crops.

Maize was the main food for the Mayans. If this failed to grow properly, there would have been catastrophic results.

Some historians also believe that diseases carried by parasites like mosquitos likely killed off large populations of the Mayans over the centuries. They point to the large number of infectious diseases—like malaria—that can thrive in rainforest environments. The Mayans would not have been immune to these maladies.

MALARIA

Malaria is a disease that is carried and spread by infected mosquitos. The earliest recorded case of malaria can be traced back two thousand years to ancient Rome, according to the study of human bones. The Romans referred to the disease as "bad air," but it later became known as marsh fever or swamp fever since mosquitoes tend to live and breed in such areas.

Malaria is responsible for the deaths of thousands of people around the world annually. The parasite travels from the mosquito's saliva in a mosquito bite. It then travels to the victim's liver, where it continues to reproduce. Normally, about ten to fifteen days after being bitten by an infected mosquito victims begin to experience vomiting, headaches, high fever, and fatigue. The worst cases can result in yellow skin, coma, and even death.

Malaria affects animals as well as humans. Because of the conditions in which malaria thrives, it isn't prolific in North America and Europe, except for in cases where travelers brought it back to their locality.

Even if the Mayans survived these rainforest diseases, it is likely that they would have suffered a lifetime of problems, including weakened immune systems.

THE ARRIVAL OF NEW DISEASES

Despite violence, warfare, famine, drought, and disease, the Mayans were not completely gone by the time the Spanish conquistadores arrived. The arrival of the Spaniards meant the arrival of European diseases that were new to the area and the Mayans. They included smallpox, typhus, influenza, measles, and yellow fever.

The Spanish conquistadores, led by Hernán Cortés, used metal weapons, wore armor, and rode horses into battle.

These diseases did a better job at eliminating the remaining Mayans than any battle or raid conducted by the conquistadores. The people had no natural resistance to these new diseases and the mortality rate was very high, sometimes as high as 90 percent. In fact, smallpox was so devastating for the Mayans that they gave it the name *mayacimil*, or "easy death." They called it that because the disease usually killed Mayans within a few days of being exposed.

Still, throughout all this, the Mayan people survived. They abandoned the cities and thoughts of empire and settled in small, nondescript agricultural communities in the jungles and highlands of places like Belize and Guatemala.

But that doesn't mean they remained safe over the years. In fact, the world's remaining Mayans would face the greatest threat to their survival during modern times: they would face racism and scorn and an attempt by the Guatemalan military to completely wipe them out.

CHAPTER 4

MODERN-DAY GENOCIDE

One of Guatemala's darkest and most shameful periods occurred only a few decades ago. At this time, the Guatemalan government tried to wipe out the Mayans once and for all. But unlike previous attacks on the Mayan people, this horrific instance would receive international support, including material support from the US government.

THE BIRTH OF GUATEMALA

By the time the Spaniards arrived in the New World in the sixteenth century, the once great and thriving Mayan Empire had basically collapsed. Gone were the vibrant cities and their powerful rulers. The Spaniards arrived to find mostly abandoned cities and people mainly scattered throughout the vast area known as Mesoamerica. Those who did remain and encounter the Spanish conquistadores were likely to fall ill from disease or die by the sword as these new invaders came with armor and steel and seemed invincible. There were even some bloody battles that accompanied the Spanish campaign to destroy Mayan culture by burning books, destroying temples, and slaughtering any who opposed the Spanish.

Guatemala won its independence in a bloodless act, a declaration called the Act of Independence of Central America. This act freed not only Guatemala, but much of Central America from Spanish rule.

But that would be the only bloodless part of the struggle for self-determination. Like many former colonies, Guatemala endured an extensive period of unrest after achieving autonomy. The time of Guatemalan instability lasted from the time it achieved independence from Spain in 1821 to after the Guatemalan genocide against the Mayans ended in 1996.

In September 1821, Guatemala, El Salvador, Honduras, Nicaragua, and Costa Rica banded together to form the Federal Republic of Central America. However, throughout their collective union, the Mexican Empire would briefly gain power over some provinces of Guatemala, and disunity between liberal and conservative factions would cause various power struggles until the union dissolved into several independent states.

From the end of the Federation in 1840 until the early twentieth century, Guatemala was highly unstable. It wasn't until US corporations and the government of the United States began to meddle in Guatemala's affairs that there was another ruler that was able to unify Guatemala. Unfortunately, for the sake of protecting American interests, US groups would install several dictators.

UNITED FRUIT COMPANY

Colonialism often takes the shape of a business based in one country overtaking the needs of the people in another. Founded in 1899, the United Fruit Company (UFC) was one example of an American corporation that was able to overtake the needs and will of Guatemalans. UFC did so by purchasing and controlling much of Guatemala's land, starting with a railroad contract in 1904. The UFC was able to become closely aligned with President Dwight D. Eisenhower, who was president between 1953 and 1961, for a few reasons. The main lobbyist for the company, Ed Whitman, was married to the president's personal assistant, and John Foster Dulles, a lawyer who represented the UFC and was on the UFC's payroll, became the secretary of state in President Eisenhower's administration. These close ties helped the UFC campaign for the US government to install Carlos Castillo Armas as Guatemala's dictator in 1954. The reason for supporting Armas was that the UFC expected him to uphold labor and land ownership laws favorable to UFC.

But the UFC wasn't only active in Guatemala. It also had operations in Cuba, Colombia, Ecuador, and the West Indies.

As of August 1984, the United Fruit Company lives on as part of Chiquita Brands International (CBI). CBI also has a history of taking part in activities that cause political instability in other countries. But even though these corporations have caused harm in the countries where they

(continued on the next page)

(continued from the previous page)

operate, they have also contributed roads, jobs, and schools to some of those countries. These positive contributions may gain some favorable sentiment toward them, even in the face of overwhelming dislike of the overbearing actions and great harm they have perpetuated.

Even when a military coup that occurred in 1944 managed to overthrow authoritarian leader Jorge Ubico, in 1954, the United States would successfully support a dictator that would bring to the Mayans a modern episode of genocide, as well as a particularly bloody civil war.

A SILENT HOLOCAUST

As was often the case, Guatemalans who were acting contrary to the desires of the US government were self-determined. Six years after the US government installed Carlos Castillo Armas as dictator, General Ydigoras Fuentes had come to power, and a failed insurgency in 1960 would herald the beginning of efforts to mobilize armed rebel forces. In 1962, the Rebel Armed Forces would emerge from those efforts. However, the revolutionaries posed no significant threat to the incumbent government.

Meanwhile, the Guatemalan government put in place counterinsurgency efforts. These efforts included the suspension of civil rights in November 1966, the formation of illegal groups whose purpose was to kill suspected dissidents or communists by 1967, nightly eight-hour curfews, and other activities meant to strengthen government power and weaken the insurgents.

The Mayan genocide, also called the Silent Holocaust, took place during this era, and lasted from the 1960s to the 1980s. Those Mayans who would be victimized were the ones who fled to the highland areas of what is now Guatemala or Chiapas, Mexico, back when the Spaniards were conquering Central American territory.

Like the Spaniards, the Guatemalan government considered the Mayans to be subhuman. Because of the civil war, the Guatemalan government felt they had a compelling reason

This map shows Guatemala. Mexico sits on the north and west border, while Belize borders Guatemala at the northeast. Honduras and El Salvador sit at Guatemala's southeast border.

to act on those sentiments. As it happened, the revolutionaries who challenged the government operated from the highlands, the area the Mayans had settled in after fleeing the Spaniards.

At first, the Guatemalan military would occasionally attack and destroy entire villages of Mayans. The Guatemalan military believed that the Mayans were supporting and helping the rebels, and they wanted to send a message. These massacres were systematically carried out against people who, even if they did have weapons, were no match for the greater firepower of the Guatemalan military. Nonetheless, these events included the slaughter of Mayan women and children. It seemed that the Guatemalan military's only goal was to destabilize any people who were even remotely threatening. They gladly continued to receive aid from a US government that was fully aware of the raids and murder of fairly unthreatening people that was taking place when it decided to back up those who committed those atrocities and everything that followed.

DEMANDING RIGHTS

The government's campaign against the Mayans would become much worse starting in 1975. By this time the Mayans had become vocal about wanting equal rights in Guatemala. They wanted their language and culture to be recognized, and they wanted a voice in government. They engaged in peaceful protests and were trying to have their demands met in a manner that did not, by any means, rely on violence. But the government saw this as a threat to its rule.

On June 30, 1981, the Armed Forces Day Parade took place. The Guatemalan Army marched during the parade in Guatemala City. This was during the period of the genocide.

In 1980, the Guatemalan army initiated Operation Sophia. This was an organized attempt to rid the country of the Mayans once and for all. Over the next few years, the army attacked and destroyed 626 Mayan villages and killed more than two hundred thousand people. Many of the victims were tortured before being killed and were buried in mass graves.

The government's strategy also included a scorched-earth policy. This meant that they not only killed the people but also burned their villages, killed any farm animals they had, polluted their water sources, violated sacred grounds, and destroyed any Mayan symbols. There was even a special unit of the army that was responsible for carrying out the genocide. The special units were known as *kabiles*.

The killings would last for thirty-six years, but they reached their most brutal and horrific point in the 1980s. Many Mayans fled to neighboring Mexico when they realized that this would be their end.

JUSTICE

Finally, after nearly four decades of warfare, the killings stopped in 1996 when the government signed a peace treaty with the insurgents. This agreement was called the Guatemalan Peace Accords.

Part of the agreement instructed the United Nations to put together a group to look into the accusations of genocide. This group would be become known as the Commission of Historical Clarification (CEH).

In 1999, only two years after being formed, the commission issued a scathing report, "Guatemala: Memory of Silence," which laid out in detail the government policy of genocide that had been carried out against the Mayan people.

The report specifically named the different groups, or tribes, of Mayans that had been targeted for extermination: they were the Ixil Mayas; the Q'anjob'al and Chuj Mayas; the K'iche' Mayas of Joyabaj, Zacualpa, and Chiché; and the Achi Mayas.

GUATEMALAN PEACE ACCORDS

Usually, the winners of a war or a conflict impose treaties or peace agreements on the group that they defeated. But the United Nations proposed a solution that all sides accepted after thirty-six years of conflict. It was time for the longest and bloodiest era in Latin American history to come to an end.

The United Nations did not declare a victor but instead tried to split the differences between the different sides. This was the same tactic the United Nations used to usher in peace

(continued on the next page)

A meeting of the United Nations. This was the group that condemned the leaders and the Guatemalan army for the slaughter of innocent and unarmed Mayans.

(continued from the previous page)

in the nearby country of El Salvador, which had also been embroiled in a long civil war.

The most important part of the peace accords, other than mandating an end to warfare, was that major revisions had to be made to the country's constitution and laws. This meant extending rights to the Mayans and an investigation into the genocide.

Many of Guatemala's leaders opposed this deal, but they eventually agreed and peace came to the countryside.

The new government of Guatemala, watched closely by human rights groups, soon started arresting those responsible and brought them to trial. In late 1998, three soldiers were the first of many to be convicted of murder and genocide. The trials continued for more than a decade as police captured those responsible.

In 2009, former military commissioner Felipe Cusanero was sentenced to 150 years in prison. Two years later, General Héctor Mario López Fuentes was caught and charged with genocide and crimes against humanity. In a tremendous victory for the victims, in 2011, four soldiers were sentenced to thirty years for every murder they committed for a total of 6,060 years each. They had been responsible for the massacre of an entire village, Dos Erres.

General Efraín Ríos Montt speaks to the press in 1982 after seizing power from President Romeo Lucas Garcia. He would later order the genocidal massacre of the Mayans.

One of the men responsible for some of the worst atrocities may have found a way to escape justice. Efraín Ríos Montt, the eighty-six-year-old former dictator of Guatemala, took advantage of immunity laws by serving several terms in Guatemala's congress. He was saved until 2012 when his term ended. That's when the government arrested him and put him on trial. He was found guilty of crimes against humanity and sentenced to eighty years in prison.

But the Constitutional Court of Guatemala overturned the conviction, so he would have to be retried. In 2015, the court ruled that he can be tried and convicted but cannot serve any time in prison because of his age and poor health.

A TIME TO HEAL

One eye-opening finding that the Commission on Historical Clarification revealed in its report was that at no time during the thirty-six years of conflict did the rebels or insurgent groups ever pose a real threat to the state, the government, or the army. The government knew that and purposely exaggerated the threat to justify sending troops into the mountains to commit genocide.

In the aftermath, young children were given certain rights in Guatemala that they did not have earlier. This is probably because soldiers targeted young Mayan children.

Overall, the Mayans are still treated as second-class citizens in Guatemala and are behind in almost every facet of society, from education to jobs to health care. Somehow, the Mayan people still exist in Guatemala, in the highlands, but they often feel like foreigners in their own land.

CHAPTER 5

LEGACY

There are still Mayans in the world, and their numbers are increasing. They continue to survive through times fraught with peril and violence because they are and always have been resilient. However, the status of the Mayans in the twenty-first century still isn't quite what it used to be.

In recent years another group of Mayan tribes have found themselves in the middle of skirmishes between government soldiers and rebels in Chiapas, Mexico. The Mayans there have suffered but there has been no evidence of another genocide.

In Honduras, many Mayans are being forced from lands they have inhabited for generations because of a growing demand for African palm oil, used in food processing and in cosmetic products. Some of the land disputes have turned deadly, leaving some Mayans hurt or killed.

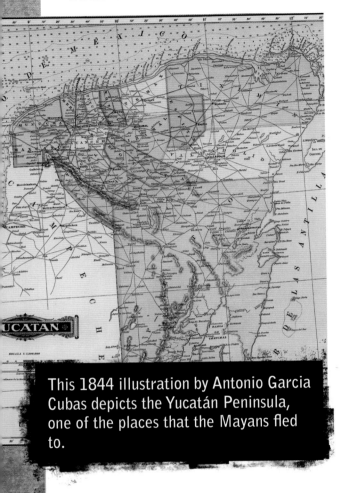

This 1844 illustration by Antonio Garcia Cubas depicts the Yucatán Peninsula, one of the places that the Mayans fled to.

THOSE WHO REMAIN

There are 6.1 million Mayans that continue to live in the highlands they have called home for thousands of years. But they also live in Mexico's Yucatán Peninsula and throughout Belize and El Salvador. Against all odds, there are roughly six million Mayans living in Central America today.

There are more than thirty Mayan groups spread out throughout what used to be known as Mesoamerica. These different groups or tribes are not able to communicate with each other. Each tribe speaks a totally different language than the other tribes, even though each language belongs to the Mayan family. Some experts in Mayan culture feel that the only way for the Mayans to continue to survive and thrive is for the people to somehow find a common language that can unite all the Mayan tribes. Then, the Mayans will have a chance to understand and embrace their proud history with

RIGOBERTA MENCHU

This symbol of hope for the Mayan people and other indigenous people was born on January 9, 1959, in Guatemala. Rigoberta Menchu was born into a poor Mayan family living in north-central Guatemala.

Menchu received some education but left school to become an activist who would speak out against the injustices the Mayans suffered in her country. Her father joined the rebel movement and was killed by government soldiers.

(continued on the next page)

015 photo depicts Rigoberta Menchu, the 1992 recipient of ɔbel Peace Prize. Here, she speaks in an interview about mass zation.

(continued from the previous page)

His death forced her to escape to safety in Mexico where she continued to raise awareness about the situation in Guatemala. Upon returning to Guatemala, she called on the courts in Spain to bring those responsible for the genocide to justice. Her reasoning was that she felt the courts in Guatemala were too crooked and could not be trusted to hold responsible parties accountable for their deeds.

In 1992, she was awarded the Nobel Peace Prize for her work in the field of social justice. She is well-known for writing a book that has been translated into numerous languages and distributed all over the world, called *My Name is Rigoberta Menchu and This Is How My Conscience Was Born.*

One of the most quoted things she said was this eloquent statement about being Mayan: "We are not myths of the past, ruins in the jungle or zoos. We are people and we want to be respected, not to be victims of intolerance and racism."

Her example and presence has helped to pave the way for other Mayans to try and integrate into mainstream politics in their respective countries. She has twice run for president in her home country but was defeated both times. There are even Mayans in Guatemala's Congress.

fewer limitations between those who interact with multiple Mayan tribes.

For the most part, Mayans are on the fringes of society, existing in some cases on the money generated from tourism. There have been cases of individual settlements that survive by farming corn and weaving textiles like blankets and dresses, and conducting trade. However, this work has fallen primarily to the women. Mayan men are often forced to leave their villages to find work elsewhere. Many have to work on plantations picking cotton or coffee when the crops are ready in order to help their families survive.

However, there are signs that the Mayan culture and civilization might be making a comeback. The Mayan population has risen in recent years despite signs that it should be dwindling. In some places the Mayan language is being taught in schools.

Perhaps there is no greater symbol of hope that the Mayans will continue to survive and perhaps even thrive again than Rigoberta Menchu. Menchu is a Guatemalan woman and Mayan activist who has been on the leading edge of calling for equal rights and equal opportunities for the Mayans, other indigenous people, and children.

DIRE STRAITS

Despite these gains, which are significant considering how far the Mayans have come, things remain dire for the majority of the Mayans. There are common issues that consistently plague

HOW YOU CAN FIGHT HATE

The way to stop hate and bigotry starts with the person in the mirror. But once you've removed racist and bigoted thoughts, feelings, and even friends from your life, there are other things to do to ensure that atrocities like the Silent Holocaust in Guatemala never happens again.

One way to get involved is to donate to one of many worthy organizations like Human Rights Watch or Stop Genocide Now. Research the various groups that exist to see which ones are agreeable. Some groups focus on awareness, while others focus on pressuring politicians to punish those responsible. There are also groups that offer assistance to victims of hate.

Those who have a particular skill can share it with afflicted people who would benefit from it. Nursing students are regularly invited on trips to the Guatemalan highlands to practice their skills and give medical attention to the Mayans. A person with a strong back can help build a well to bring fresh water to a village or help with some other project that has a clear need and that people have requested.

Just about every organization needs volunteers and community activists. For example, the group United to End Genocide is always looking for people to get involved. That group even lists ways to help, including asking local legislators to support certain legislative action or showing a film, such as *Hotel Rwanda,* and then hosting a discussion afterward.

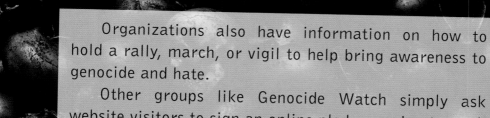

Organizations also have information on how to hold a rally, march, or vigil to help bring awareness to genocide and hate.

Other groups like Genocide Watch simply ask website visitors to sign an online pledge vowing to work toward and support efforts to end genocide everywhere. It can be that simple.

the Mayans as well as other indigenous people throughout the world. They are unemployment, poverty, bigotry, lower wages, and being made the scapegoat during times of political unrest.

Much like the Mayans that disappeared from the ancient cities before the Spaniards arrived, the Mayans of today also generally suffer from hunger. The United Nations has set the minimum standard for daily caloric intake at about 2,500 calories. However, many Mayans survive on only about five hundred calories a day. And with a diet consisting of primarily corn products, there is very little protein consumed. According to the United Nations Development Program, close to 60 percent of Mayan children suffer from malnutrition and forty out of every one thousand infants do not survive.

Overall, the life expectancy for Mayans is only forty-four years. In the United States, the life expectancy is seventy-nine years.

Change, both good and bad, can happen very slowly. Maybe there is hope for the Mayans. As University of Arizona, professor

Guatemalan indigenous congresswoman Catarina Pastor of the Patriotic Party addresses the Guatemalan Congress on October 9, 2012.

of Latin American studies Elizabeth Oglesby says maybe the biggest hope for positive change is that people have finally recognized just how much the Mayans have suffered over the years:

"There is a public recognition in Guatemala that the Mayan community suffered the worst of the atrocities and that there is a historical injustice that has been done against the Mayan community... I think that is a public recognition that didn't exist a generation ago, so there is lots of discussion about that. Many Mayan leaders have risen to positions of some prominence. You have Mayans in Congress, you have Mayan leaders as government ministers. So there is progress in this sense, but it's been uneven and it's been insufficient."

TIMELINE

11000 BCE The first hunter-gatherers come to the Mayan highlands and lowlands.

2600 BCE The first Mayan cities are formed.

400 BCE Stone-carved solar calendars begin to be used throughout the Mayan Empire.

100 BCE The city of Teotihuacan is founded. It soon becomes the center of the Mayan Empire.

400 CE The Mayan Empire begins to disintegrate in some areas of the highlands.

500 CE Tikal becomes the new major city in Mayan culture and new ideas are born, including advanced weapons, taking prisoners, and human sacrifice.

600 CE The city of Teotihuacan is burned down by an unidentified group.

751 CE Many of the long-standing alliances and agreements with other civilizations and trading partners begin to break down.

869 CE For the first time in more than three hundred years the city of Tikal stops growing. There is no new construction and this marks the beginning of the end for the city.

1200 CE Northern Mayan cities are mysteriously abandoned.

1283 CE Mayapan becomes the capital city of the Yucatán area.

1461 CE After a rebellion within the city, residents abandon Mayapan.

1511 CE Spaniard Gonzalo Guerrero is shipwrecked and joins the Mayan people in the fight against Spanish invaders.

1519 CE Spanish explorer Hernán Cortés explores the Yucatán area.

1960 CE Guatemalan army forces begin systematically killing Mayan citizens.

1995 CE The rebel forces call for a ceasefire in the conflict.

1995 CE The United Nations criticizes Guatemala for human rights abuses.

2004 CE Former military leader Efraín Ríos Montt is placed under house arrest for ordering the massacre of Mayan villagers.

2006 CE A Spanish judge issues an arrest warrant for Montt and others for atrocities committed against the Mayans.

2011 CE Four former Guatemalan soldiers are found guilty for their part in the massacre of a Mayan village. They are the first to be held accountable for human rights abuses in the genocide against the Mayans.

GLOSSARY

anthropologist A professional who studies human societies.

communism A political ideology in which the government owns all property and wealth is distributed based on need.

conquerors Invaders who take over the rule of land that did not previously belong to them.

deforestation To cut down the trees in a forest.

denizen A person who lives in a country. This person may be a citizen or an immigrant.

depleted Something that has been used until it is all gone.

destabilize To make something unstable; to remove elements of a society like jobs or resources that made it functional.

elaborate A thing that involves many details.

eschatologist A person who studies religious beliefs concerning the end of the world.

ethnic cleansing To force people of a certain collective identity (ethnicity, race, or religion) to leave a place where they were known to live, or to kill them.

fertilizer Nutrients one adds to land in order to make the soil healthy.

foundation A solid basis for something.

holistic Taking all parts of something into consideration.

holocaust Large-scale slaughter or destruction of people.

incumbent The person or group that holds political power.

indigenous People that are native to a place.

insurgency An uprising that seeks to illegally replace one government with another.

material support Things like food, weapons, or plans one supplies to help another group or person. Material support to a terrorist is itself considered an act of disobeying the law.

parasites Organisms that feed off of others and cause harm.

retaliation Attempting to harm someone as revenge after they have harmed or attempted to harm you.

self-determination The sentiment of one country's people desiring self-rule without owing allegiance, money, or any other type of favor to another country.

stagnant Something that has reached a period of very slow or stalled growth.

superstitious Acting strangely in an attempt to prevent things that one doesn't understand from happening.

systematically An intentional and well-planned way for one or many branches of a government to do something that is meant to achieve some goal.

understatement A statement that describes something as much less important or serious than it actually is, for example, to say a mortal wound is "just a scratch."

vassal A person or group that is dominated by another.

American Indian Genocide Museum
PO Box 230452
Houston, Texas 77223
(281) 841-3028
Website: http://www.aigenom.org
Facebook: @AmericanIndianGenocideMuseum
Twitter: @theaigm
Youtube: TheAIGM
This museum seeks to educate visitors about the genocide
European settlers perpetuated against Native Americans
throughout the Americas.

Canadian Lawyers for International Human Rights
66 Wellington Street West
PO Box 1074
Toronto, ON M5K 1A0
Canada
Website: http://claihr.ca
Facebook: @claihr
Twitter: @CLAIHRA
This charitable organization of lawyers offers its services for
human rights issues.

The Center for Justice and Accountability
One Hallidie Plaza, Suite 406
San Francisco, CA 94102
(415) 544-0444
Website: http://cja.org/
Facebook: @CenterForJusticeAndAccountability

Twitter: @cja_news
This organization works to end the abuses of groups who
  violate the human rights of other groups or individuals.

Genocide Watch
PO Box 809
Washington, DC 20044
(703) 448-0222
Website: http://www.genocidewatch.org
Twitter: @genocide_watch
This international group's mission is to prevent and punish
  those responsible for genocide.

Human Rights Watch
350 Fifth Avenue, 34th floor
New York, NY 10118-3299
(212) 290-4700
Website: https://www.hrw.org
Twitter: @hrw
This international fact-finding group reports on human rights
  abuses.

Montreal Institute for Genocide and Human Rights Studies
  (MIGS)
1250 Guy Street
Montreal, QC H3G 1M8
Canada
(514) 848-2424 ext. 5729 or 2404
Website: http://www.concordia.ca/research/migs
Facebook: @migs.montreal
Twitter: @MIGSinstitute
Youtube: @DMAPLab MIGS

This group's goal is to prevent genocide and ethnic cleansing and to encourage peace.

WEBSITES

Because of the changing nature of internet links, Rosen Publishing has developed an online list of websites related to the subject of this book. This site is updated regularly. Please use this link to access this list:

http://www.rosenlinks.com/BWGE/Maya

FOR FURTHER READING

Ardren, Traci, and Scott R. Hutson. *Social Experience of Childhood in Ancient Mesoamerica.* Boulder, CO: University Press Of Colorado, 2015.

Carlsen, William. *Jungle of Stone: the True Story of Two Men, Their Extraordinary Journey, and the Discovery of the Lost Civilization of the Maya.* New York, NY: William Morrow, 2016.

Carmack, Robert M., Janine Gasco, and Gary H. Gossen. *The Legacy of Mesoamerica: History and Culture of a Native American Civilization.* Abingdon, UK: Taylor and Francis Group, 2016.

Cruden, Alex. *Genocide and Persecution: El Salvador and Guatemala.* Detroit, MI: Greenhaven Press, 2013.

Grube, Nikolai. *Maya: Divine Kings of the Rainforest.* London, UK: H.F. Ullman, 2016.

Laughton, Timothy. *Exploring the Life, Myth, and Art of the Maya* (Civilizations of the World). New York, NY: Rosen Publishing, 2012.

MacAllister, Carlota, and Diane M Nelson. *War by Other Means: Aftermath in Post-Genocide Guatemala.* Durham, NC: Duke University Press, 2013.

Murphy, John. *Gods & Goddesses of the Inca, Maya, and Aztec Civilizations* (Gods and Goddesses of Mythology). New York, NY: Britannica Educational Publishing, 2015.

Nelson, Diane M. *Who Counts? The Mathematics of Death and Life After Genocide.* Durham, NC: Duke University Press, 2015.

Powell, Jillian. *The Maya.* London, UK: Franklin Watts, 2016.

Annenberg Learner Teacher Resources. "Why Do Civilizations Fall?" Retrieved March 1, 2017. https://www.learner.org/exhibits/collapse/mayans.html.

Burt, Jo-Marie. "In Guatemala, Victims Commemorate the Third Anniversary of the Genocide Verdict." Huffington Post. Retrieved March 31, 2017. http://www.huffingtonpost.com/jomarie-burt/in-guatemala-victims-comm_b_9905686.html.

Canby, Peter. "The Maya Genocide Trial." *New Yorker*, May 3, 2013. http://www.newyorker.com/news/daily-comment/the-maya-genocide-trial.

Demarest, Arthur A, and M.-Charlotte Arnauld Alain Breton, ed. "The Collapse of the Classic Maya Kingdoms of the Southwestern Petén: Implications for the End of Classic Maya Civilization." *Millenary Maya Societies: Past Crises and Resilience.* Mesoweb, 2013. http://www.mesoweb.com/publications/MMS/MMS.pdf.

Hays, Brook. "Archeologists Shed New Light on Collapse of the Maya Civilization." United Press International, January 23, 2017. http://www.upi.com/Science_News/2017/01/23/Archaeologists-shed-new-light-on-collapse-of-Mayan-civilization/6631485206072/.

History. "Maya: Facts and Summary." Retrieved on March 5, 2017. http://www.history.com/topics/maya.

History. "Mayan Scientific Achievements." November 14, 2015. http://www.history.com/topics/mayan-scientific-achievements.

Holocaust Museum Houston. "Genocide in Guatemala." Retrieved on March 3, 2017. https://www.hmh.org/la_Genocide_Guatemala.shtml.

Inomata, Takeshi. "Maya Collapse and Modern Society." *New York Times*, April 14, 2011. https://scientistatwork.blogs. nytimes.com/2011/04/14/maya-collapse-and-modern-society/?_r=0.

Kiger, Patrick. "Did the Mayan Civilization End Because of Climate Change?" HowStuffWorks, December 3, 2012. http:// science.howstuffworks.com/environmental/green-science/ climate-change-end-mayan-civilization1.htm.

NASA. "The Fall of the Maya: They Did it to Themselves." October 6, 2009. https://science.nasa.gov/science-news/ science-at-nasa/2009/06oct_maya.

Newitz, Annalee. "What Really Destroyed the Maya Civilization?" Gizmodo, February 24, 2012. http://io9. gizmodo.com/5886796/did-mild-weather-really-destroy-the-mayan-empire.

Pritchett, Dan. "An Ancient Maya Legacy." *Houston Chronicle*, March 29, 2008. http://www.chron.com/life/travel/article/ An-ancient-Maya-legacy-1571663.php.

Pruitt, Sarah. "What Caused the Maya Collapse? Archeologists Uncover New Clues." History, January 25, 2017. http:// www.history.com/news/what-caused-the-maya-collapse-archaeologists-uncover-new-clues.

Sanford, Victoria. "Violence and Genocide in Guatemala." Yale University. Retrieved on March 2, 2017. http://gsp.yale.edu/ case-studies/guatemala/violence-and-genocide-guatemala.

Stromberg, Joseph. "Why Did the Mayan Civilization Collapse?" Smithsonian, August 23, 2012. http://www. smithsonianmag.com/science-nature/why-did-the-mayan-civilization-collapse-a-new-study-points-to-deforestation-and-climate-change-30863026/.

Vankin, Jonathan. "Why Was the Mayan Civilization Destroyed?" Inquisitr, December 29, 2014. http://www.

inquisitr.com/1714088/mayan-civilization-destroyed-blue-hole/.

Voice of America. "Guatemala's Mayan Indians Endure Poverty." October 27, 2009. http://www.voanews.com/a/a-13-2007-11-16-voa47-66528207/553747.html.

Voice of America. "Survivors Remember Guatemalan Genocide." September 6, 2015. http://learningenglish.voanews.com/a/survivors-remember-gautemalan-genocide/2946595.html.

Wylie, Robin. "Severe Droughts Explain the Mysterious Fall of the Mayan Empire." BBC, February 22, 2016. http://www.bbc.com/earth/story/20160222-severe-droughts-explain-the-mysterious-fall-of-the-maya.

INDEX

ABOUT THE AUTHOR

John A. Torres is a journalist and writer who has written more than sixty books. His reporting has taken him to Indonesia, India, Zambia, Italy, Mexico, Haiti, and many other countries. When Torres is not writing, he enjoys reading, fishing, spending time with his family, and playing music with his band, The Hemingways.

PHOTO CREDITS